VOCAL SELECTIONS

20th ANNIVERSARY

John TRAVOLTA · Olivia NEWTON-JOHN

GREASE is *still* the word

PARAMOUNT PICTURES PRESENTS A ROBERT STIGWOOD/ALLAN CARR PRODUCTION JOHN TRAVOLTA OLIVIA NEWTON-JOHN "GREASE" AND STOCKARD CHANNING AS RIZZO

WITH SPECIAL GUEST APPEARANCES BY EVE ARDEN, FRANKIE AVALON, JOAN BLONDELL, EDD BYRNES, SID CAESAR, ALICE GHOSTLEY, DODY GOODMAN, SHA-NA-NA SCREENPLAY BY BRONTE WOODARD

ADAPTATION BY ALLAN CARR BASED ON THE ORIGINAL MUSICAL BY JIM JACOBS AND WARREN CASEY PRODUCED ON THE BROADWAY STAGE BY KENNETH WAISSMAN AND MAXINE FOX IN ASSOCIATION WITH ANTHONY D'AMATO CHOREOGRAPHY BY PATRICIA BIRCH

PRODUCED BY ROBERT STIGWOOD AND ALLAN CARR DIRECTED BY RANDAL KLEISER

PG PARENTAL GUIDANCE SUGGESTED
SOME MATERIAL MAY NOT BE SUITABLE FOR CHILDREN

SOUNDTRACK ON POLYDOR CDs AND CASSETTES www.greasemovie.com

ISBN 0-7935-9438-3

HAL·LEONARD® CORPORATION
7777 W. BLUEMOUND RD. P.O. BOX 13819 MILWAUKEE, WI 53213

Visit Hal Leonard Online at
www.halleonard.com

20th ANNIVERSARY

John TRAVOLTA Olivia NEWTON-JOHN

GREASE is *still* the word

CONTENTS

GREASE

Words and Music by
BARRY GIBB

Moderately, with a beat

I solve my prob-lems and I see the light. We got a

lov-in' thing.__ We got-ta feed it right.____ There ain't no dan-ger we can

go too far.__ We start be-liev-in' now that we can be who we are.__ Grease is the word.__

HOPELESSLY DEVOTED TO YOU

Words and Music by
JOHN FARRAR

YOU'RE THE ONE THAT I WANT

Words and Music by
JOHN FARRAR

SANDY

Words and Music by SCOTT SIMON
and LOUIS ST. LOUIS

Freely

Strand-ed at the drive-in. Brand-ed a fool. What will they say Mon-day at school?

Medium Rock beat

BEAUTY SCHOOL DROPOUT

Lyric and Music by WARREN CASEY
and JIM JACOBS

LOOK AT ME, I'M SANDRA DEE

Lyric and Music by WARREN CASEY
and JIM JACOBS

Look at me. I'm San- dra Dee,
Watch it! Hey, I'm Dor- is Day.
As for you, Troy Don- a- hue,

lous- y with vir- gin- i- ty.
I was not brought up that way.
I know not what you wan- na do.

Won't go to bed till I'm le- gal- ly wed. I
Won't come a- cross. E- ven Rock Hud- son lost his
You got your crust! I'm no ob- ject of lust. I'm

SUMMER NIGHTS

Lyric and Music by WARREN CASEY
and JIM JACOBS

46

GREASED LIGHTNIN'

Lyric and Music by WARREN CASEY
and JIM JACOBS

Go Greased Light - nin'. You're coast - in' through the heat lap trial.

You are su - preme. The chicks - 'll

cream for Greased Light - nin'. We'll get some

Light - nin'.

IT'S RAINING ON PROM NIGHT

Lyric and Music by WARREN CASEY
and JIM JACOBS

BLUE MOON

Words by LORENZ HART
Music by RICHARD RODGERS

my arms could ev - er hold.

I heard some - bod - y

whis - per, "Please, a - dore

me." But when I looked,

MOONING

Lyric and Music by WARREN CASEY
and JIM JACOBS

ALONE AT THE DRIVE-IN MOVIE

Lyric and Music by WARREN CASEY
and JIM JACOBS

ROCK AND ROLL IS HERE TO STAY

Words and Music by
DAVID WHITE

THOSE MAGIC CHANGES

Lyric and Music by WARREN CASEY
and JIM JACOBS

HOUND DOG

Words and Music by JERRY LEIBER
and MIKE STOLLER

Fast Rock 'n' Roll beat

You ain't noth-in' but a hound dog, __ cry-in' all the time. You ain't noth-in' but a hound dog, __ cry-in' all the time. Well, __ you ain't nev-er caught a rab-bit, and you ain't no friend of mine. __

To Coda

BORN TO HAND JIVE

Lyric and Music by WARREN CASEY
and JIM JACOBS

Medium tempo, in 2

Be -

fore I was born, late ___ one night,
bare - ly walk when I milked a cow.

my pa - pa said, "Ev - 'ry - thing's all right." ___
When I was three, I pushed a plow. ___

Tears on My Pillow

Words and Music by SYLVESTER BRADFORD
and AL LEWIS

You don't re-mem-ber me,___ but I re-mem-ber you.___
If we could start a-new,___ I would-n't hes-i-tate.___

'Twas not so long a-go___ you___ broke my heart in two.___
I'd glad-ly take you back___ and___ tempt the hands of fate.___

FREDDY, MY LOVE

Lyric and Music by WARREN CASEY
and JIM JACOBS

ROCK 'N' ROLL PARTY QUEEN

Lyric and Music by WARREN CASEY
and JIM JACOBS

THERE ARE WORSE THINGS I COULD DO

Lyric and Music by WARREN CASEY
and JIM JACOBS

There are worse things _ I could do than go with a boy or two.

E-ven though the _ neigh-bor-hood _ thinks I'm trash-y _ and no

LOVE IS A MANY-SPLENDORED THING

Words by PAUL FRANCIS WEBSTER
Music by SAMMY FAIN

WE GO TOGETHER

Lyric and Music by WARREN CASEY
and JIM JACOBS

We go to-geth-er,__ like ra-ma la-ma la-ma ka ding-a da ding-a dong,

re-mem-bered for-ev-er__ as shoo-bop sha wad-da wad-da yip-pi-ty boom__ de boom.

LOOK AT ME, I'M SANDRA DEE
(Reprise)

Lyric and Music by WARREN CASEY
and JIM JACOBS

scared and un-sure, a poor man's _____ San-dra Dee. _____